INCREDIBLE
SCIENCE

First published in 2012 by
Miles Kelly Publishing Ltd
Harding's Barn, Bardfield End Green,
Thaxted, Essex, CM6 3PX, UK

Copyright © Miles Kelly Publishing Ltd 2011

© 2012 Discovery Communications, LLC.
Discovery Explore Your World™ and the
Discovery Explore Your World™ logo are
trademarks of Discovery Communications, LLC,
used under license. All rights reserved.
yourdiscovery.com

10 9 8 7 6 5 4 3 2 1

Publishing Director Belinda Gallagher
Creative Director Jo Cowan
Managing Editors Amanda Askew,
  Rosie McGuire
Managing Designer Simon Lee
Proofreaders Carly Blake, Claire Philip
Production Manager Elizabeth Collins
Image Manager Liberty Newton
Reprographics Stephan Davis

ISBN 978-1-84810-509-6

Printed in China

British Library Cataloguing-in-Publication Data
A catalogue record for this book is available
from the British Library

Made with paper from a sustainable forest

www.mileskelly.net
info@mileskelly.net

www.factsforprojects.com

ACKNOWLEDGMENTS

The publishers would like to thank the following sources for the use
of their photographs:

KEY Getty Images=GI, naturepl.com/Nature Picture Library=NPL,
Photolibrary=P, Rex Features=RF, Science Photo Library=SPL, Shutterstock=S
t=top, a=above, b=bottom/below, c=center, l=left, r=right, f=far, m=main,
bg=background

COVER EYE OF SCIENCE/SPL BACK COVER photostockar/S 1 Rashevska
Nataliia/S 2 Pedro Nogueira/S 3(bg) lolloj/S (strip, left to right) James
Doss/S, Dmitri Melnik/S, Kheng Guan Toh/S, MichaelTaylor/S, Vakhrushev
Pavel/S 4–5 A 6–7 David Scharf/SPL 6(tl) Pedro Nogueira/S, (tr) NASA-JPL,
(bl) Lane V. Erickson/S, (b, l–r) Top Photo Group/RF 7(tl) Pedro Nogueira/S,
(bl) James Balog/Aurora Photos/Corbis, (r, t–b) oku/S, David Arts/S, Dmitri
Melnik/S, Sergey Kamshylin/S, Andrey Burmakin/S, (frame)
Phase4Photography/S 8–9(m) NASA/GI, (b) Joseph C Dovala/P 8(l) Edward
Kinsman/SPL, (c) Abel Tumik/S, (b, panel) Matthias Pahl/S, (b, chain)
Henry Nowick/S, (r) Phase4Photography/S 9(l) E.R.Degginger/SPL,
(r, t–b) Melli/S, Vakhrushev Pavel/S, Arsgera/S, ArtmannWitte/S
10–1(bg) lolloj/S 10(m) GI, (t) Eye of Science/SPL, (bl) Nicemonkey/S,
(br) Lawrence Berkeley National Laboratory/SPL 11(tl) NASA/SPL, (tr) RF,
(bm) Innespace Productions/SEABREACHER, (bl) Dmitri Mihhailov/S,
(br) Gwoeii/S 12–3(bg) dinadesign/S, (frame) ivn3da/S, (c) adziohiciek/S,
(ice cubes) Alex Staroseltsev/S 12(tr) NASA/Science Faction/Corbis,
(bl) Vitaly Raduntsev/S, (br) SPL 13(tl) Patrick Landmann/SPL, (tr) Ria
Novosti/SPL, (tr, frame) Hintau Aliaksei, (bl) Diego Barucco/S, (br) Yva
Momatiuk & John Eastcott/GI 14–5(bg) Zinatova Olga/S, (c) Gordan/S,
(b) Sergey Mironov/S, (t) NASA-JPL 14(l) Edward Kinsman/SPL, (r) Jean-Luc
& Françoise Ziegler/P 15(t) NASA-GSFC, (bl) NASA-JPL, (br) NASA/WMAP
Science Team/SPL 16–7(bg, wood) Ford Photography/S, (bg, book) Valentin
Agapov/S, (doodles) Bukhavets Mikhail/S, (masking tape) Studio DMM
Photography, Designs & Art/S, (frames) Phase4Photography/S 16(t) NASA-
MSFC, (b) NASA-JPL 17(tr) Viktar Malyshchyts/S, (r) happydancing/S
18–9(m) Tony Craddock/SPL 18(b) J.C. Revy, ISM/SPL 19 Volker
Springel/Max Planck Institute for Astrophysics/SPL 20–1(bg) Kheng Guan
Toh/S, (atoms) Johan Swanepoel/S, (molecules) Serdar Duran/S 20(l) Steve
Gschmeissner/SPL, (tr) David McCarthy/SPL, (br) Susumu Nishinaga/SPL
21(t) Dr Gary Gaugler/SPL, (cl) Dr Linda Stannard, UCT/SPL,
(cr) Omikron/SPL, (b) Jan Kaliciak/S 22(t) Eye of science/SPL, (c) Ower and
Syred/SPL, (b) SPL 23(tl) Jan Hinsch/SPL, (tr) Susumu Nishinaga/SPL,
(bl) Steve Gschmeissner/SPL, (br) Astrid & Hanns-Frieder Michler/SPL
24(bg) argus/S, (m) Thierry Berrod, Mona Lisa Production/SPL, (b) Bristish
Museum/Munoz-Yague/SPL 25(m) Stephen & Donna O'Meara/SPL,
(tl) Jochen Tack/P, (tr) Augusto Cabral/S, (bl) Smit/S
26–7(m) Anakaopress/Look at sciences/SPL 26(b) optimarc/S
27(t) Stephen Alvarez/GI, (c) Carsten Peter/GI, (b) Jeff Rotman/NPL
28–9(t) shelbysupercars.com, (b) David J. Cross/P 28 GI 29 NASA/SPL
30(bg, pink) Panos Karapanagiotis/S, (bg, writing) Inga Nielsen/S,
(tl) National Library of Medicine/SPL, (tr) Dmitrijs Bindemanis/S,
(cl) Library of Congress/digital version by Science Faction,
(bl) Bettmann/Corbis, (br) Dominik Michálek/S 31(tl) Jacqueline Abromeit,
(tr) RF, (cl) Bettmann/Corbis, (bl) Graeme Dawes/S, (bc) NASA-MSFC,
(br) Reuters/Corbis 32–3(m) Russell Kightley/SPL
32 NASA/ESA/STSCI/J.Kenney & E.Yale, Yale University/SPL 33 Chandra
X-ray Observatory/NASA/SPL 34–5(bg) David Parker/SPL, (clockwise
starting bl) Christophe Vander Eecken/Reporters/SPL, Adam Hart-Davis/SPL,
Tim Wright/Corbis, optimarc/S, Sylverarts/S, Emilio Naranjo/epa/Corbis
36–7(border) gorica/S 36(tl) INSAGO/S, (cl) R-studio/S, (bl) GI
37(tl) Christophe Boisvieux/Corbis, (bl) Time & Life Pictures/GI,
(r) Omikron/SPL 38–9 Jose Antonio Peñas/SPL(c) T Carrafa/Newspix/RF,
(r) Anan Kaewkhammul/S

All other photographs are from: Corel, digitalSTOCK, digitalvision,
Dreamstime.com, Fotolia.com, iStockphoto.com, John Foxx, PhotoAlto,
PhotoDisc, PhotoEssentials, PhotoPro, Stockbyte

Every effort has been made to acknowledge the source and copyright
holder of each picture. The publishers apologise for any unintentional
errors or omissions.

INCREDIBLE
SCIENCE

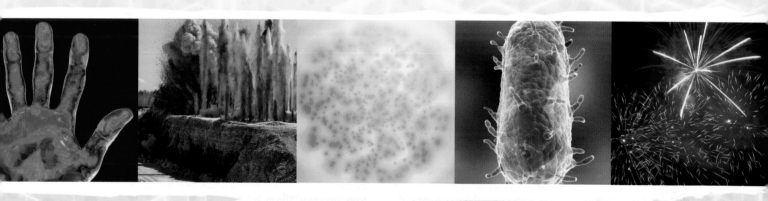

John Farndon
Consultant: Clive Gifford

Miles Kelly

CONTENTS

◀ The power of a scanning electron microscope (SEM) homes in on the head of a tiny fruit fly, showing the 800 separate lenses that make up each of its two compound eyes.

Big BANGS

Explosions are the most powerful events in the Universe, capable of suddenly blasting apart anything from a rock to an entire giant star. They occur when heat, chemical, or nuclear reactions cause a dramatic and almost instantaneous expansion of gases. Some giant explosions, such as supernovae and volcanoes, occur naturally, but man-made explosions can also be very powerful.

Exploding star

The biggest explosion in the Universe is a supernova—the explosion that ends the life of a supergiant star. It may only be visible for a week, but can be seen far across the Universe, as bright as a galaxy of 100 billion stars.

▼ The Crab Nebula is the remnants of a supernova witnessed by Chinese astronomers in AD 1054.

Blow me down!

To demolish a building without damaging anything nearby, engineers have to make it implode (explode inward). To do this, they place explosive charges in carefully chosen weak points in the building, then set them off in a particular sequence.

▲ Experts need to place explosives very carefully to bring down an unwanted building, such as this 18-story apartment block in Shenyang, China.

Death trap

Land mines are bombs that can be buried just beneath the surface of the ground. Packed with a chemical called Trinitrotoluene (TNT), a land mine explodes by detonation—a powerful shock wave rushes through it, turning all the TNT almost instantly to gas. The gas expands violently, causing terrible damage. A detonator (a tiny explosive device inside the mine) triggers the explosion. Detonators are designed to be triggered when someone steps on the mine or drives a vehicle nearby.

EXPLOSIVE STRENGTH

The power of explosions is often measured in comparison to TNT by weight.

ITEM	POWER
1. Large hand grenade	3 oz (85 g) TNT
2. World War II bomb	6 lb (2.7 kg) TNT
3. "Bunker-buster" bomb	1 ton TNT
4. Hiroshima atom bomb	15 kilotons (15,000 tons) TNT
5. Hydrogen bomb	50 megatons (25 million tons) TNT
6. Mount Toba eruption	85 megatons TNT
7. Supernova	1,000 trillion trillion tons TNT

▶ An entire rock face in a quarry is blasted away by a line of simultaneous explosions.

Volcanic violence

The VEI (Volcanic Explosivity Index) rates the power of explosive volcanic eruptions on a scale from 0 to 8. The Mount St. Helens eruption of 1980 had a VEI of 5. When Mount Toba in Indonesia erupted around 75,000 years ago, it had a VEI of 8, so it was 10,000 times more powerful than Mount St. Helens and was one of the largest explosions on Earth, ever.

▼ Volcanic eruptions are the most powerful natural explosions on Earth.

Rock blast

To blast rock from the ground, quarries usually use dynamite. Invented by Swedish chemist Alfred Nobel (1833–1896), dynamite was the first High Explosive, and consists of sticks of sawdust soaked in nitroglycerin and wrapped in paper. Nitroglycerin contains so much oxygen that it detonates easily when heated. Typically, the heat source is a current of electricity running through a wire set into the dynamite.

Chemical Clash

When a candle burns, metal goes rusty, or a cake rises in the oven, a chemical reaction is taking place. When chemicals meet and react, they change each other to form new chemicals. But not all chemical encounters are quite so gentle.

CHEMICAL REACTIONS ARE CONSTANTLY TAKING PLACE WITHIN THE 100 TRILLION OR SO LIVING CELLS INSIDE YOUR BODY, SO THERE MAY BE MORE THAN 400 BILLION REACTIONS TAKING PLACE INSIDE YOU EVERY SECOND!

Exploding pop

Dropping Mentos mints into cola makes the drink suddenly fizz up in a fountain of froth. The Mentos react chemically with the cola, instantly creating bubbles of carbon dioxide gas, which turn the cola into a gushing foam. Other substances create bubbles in soft drinks, but the chemicals in Mentos make the reaction especially dramatic.

▲ Rusting corrodes tough steel into flaky, brown iron oxide as it reacts with oxygen in the air.

▲ Mentos are covered in minute pits that act as nucleation sites— places that concentrate gas formation.

Acid danger

Strong acids are dangerous chemicals because they react so powerfully. Acids contain hydrogen, and when mixed with water the hydrogen atoms are turned loose as highly reactive "ions." Splashed on skin, acids can cause terrible burns by absorbing water in a reaction that creates a lot of heat. Strong acids can also dissolve metals.

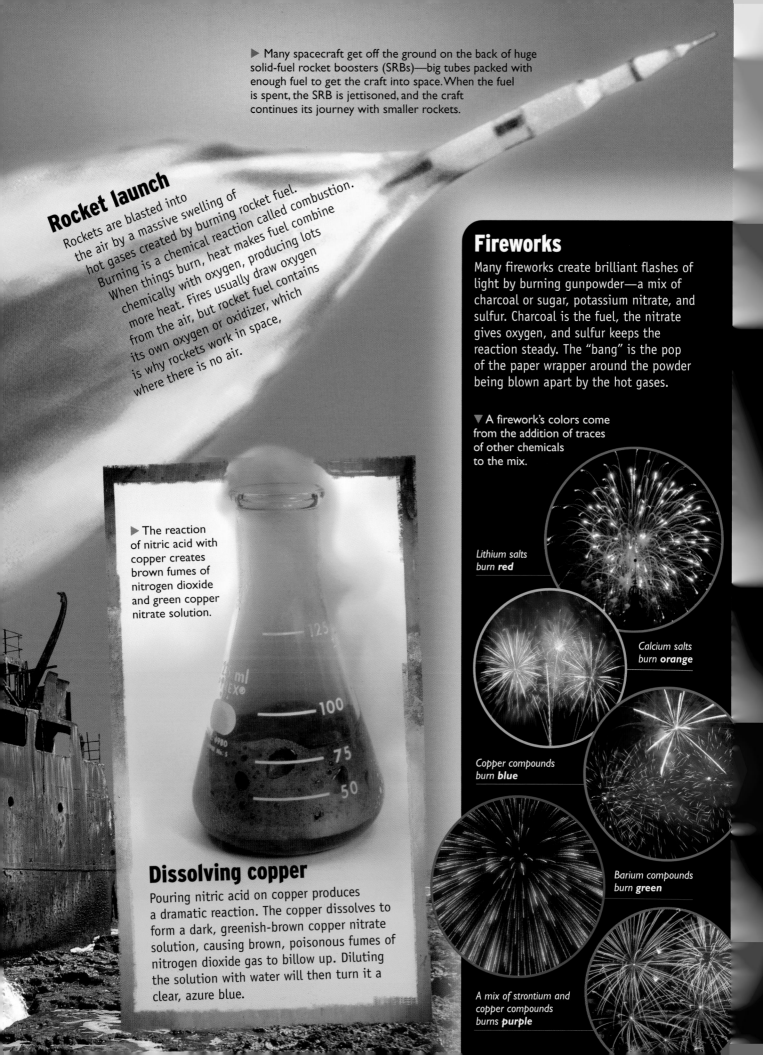

▶ Many spacecraft get off the ground on the back of huge solid-fuel rocket boosters (SRBs)—big tubes packed with enough fuel to get the craft into space. When the fuel is spent, the SRB is jettisoned, and the craft continues its journey with smaller rockets.

Rocket launch

Rockets are blasted into the air by a massive swelling of hot gases created by burning rocket fuel. Burning is a chemical reaction called combustion. When things burn, heat makes fuel combine chemically with oxygen, producing lots more heat. Fires usually draw oxygen from the air, but rocket fuel contains its own oxygen or oxidizer, which is why rockets work in space, where there is no air.

Fireworks

Many fireworks create brilliant flashes of light by burning gunpowder—a mix of charcoal or sugar, potassium nitrate, and sulfur. Charcoal is the fuel, the nitrate gives oxygen, and sulfur keeps the reaction steady. The "bang" is the pop of the paper wrapper around the powder being blown apart by the hot gases.

▼ A firework's colors come from the addition of traces of other chemicals to the mix.

Lithium salts burn **red**

Calcium salts burn **orange**

Copper compounds burn **blue**

Barium compounds burn **green**

A mix of strontium and copper compounds burns **purple**

▶ The reaction of nitric acid with copper creates brown fumes of nitrogen dioxide and green copper nitrate solution.

Dissolving copper

Pouring nitric acid on copper produces a dramatic reaction. The copper dissolves to form a dark, greenish-brown copper nitrate solution, causing brown, poisonous fumes of nitrogen dioxide gas to billow up. Diluting the solution with water will then turn it a clear, azure blue.

Wonder MATERIALS

Natural materials such as diamond and silk can be incredibly tough. But now scientists are creating a range of entirely man-made wonder materials. Some are incredibly light, others are incredibly strong, and some are both.

◄ The high-strength carbon fibers inside CRP help to absorb pressure. In a pole-vaulter's pole, CRP's combination of strength and flexibility gives a vaulter extra lift as it springs straight.

Carbon power

By embedding long fibers made of carbon in plastics, scientists make a material called carbon reinforced plastic (CRP). The plastic keeps it very light, but the fibers give it both strength and flexibility—perfect for the light, strong springiness needed for a pole-vaulter's pole. CRP is known as a "composite" because it combines plastic and carbon.

Jelly light

Aerogels are materials so light that they almost seem to float. Gels are jellylike materials that are mostly liquid. Aerogels are made by sucking liquid out of a gel and replacing it with gas. The gas filling not only makes aerogels amazingly light, but also very good barriers to heat.

CARBON FIBERS ARE FOUR TIMES STRONGER THAN STEEL WHEN PULLED, YET JUST ONE QUARTER OF THE WEIGHT.

► Aerogel stops the heat of the bunsen burner flame reaching the flower entirely.

▶ The LCROSS mission smashed a rocket with a wurtzite boron nitride nose into the Moon deliberately to throw up dust for scientists to analyze.

Tough titanium

Alloys are created by adding materials to a metal. Alloys of aluminum and magnesium are tough and light—which is why they are used to build aircraft. But the heat generated as high-speed jets tear through the air may be too much for aluminum alloys. So the fastest jets, such as the *F22 Raptor*, are made mostly from incredibly tough, superlight titanium alloys.

Super strong

Wurtzite boron nitride is the world's hardest material—harder even than diamond. It is used wherever materials need to be really, really tough and cost doesn't matter—from the heads of oil drills to the tips of "bunker-busting" bombs.

▲ With a superlight, superstrong titanium alloy fuselage (main body), the *F22 Raptor* can fly at speeds of up to 1,500 mph (2,400 km/h).

▶ The *Seabreacher* is a submersible made of Kevlar. It is so light and strong that it can burst out of the water like a dolphin.

The toughest threads

In 1961, DuPont chemist Stephanie Kwolek (b. 1923) discovered how to spin fibers from liquid chemicals such as oil. These "aramid" fibers are amazingly strong—threads of the aramid fiber Kevlar are five times stronger than steel. Kevlar has many applications, from helping to make puncture-resistant bicycle tires to strengthening cables used in suspension bridges.

▶ The fibers of Kevlar (a modified form of nylon) are incredibly tough for their weight, so they are used to make stabproof and bulletproof vests.

Deep
FREEZE

Freezing point, when water turns to ice, might seem pretty cold, but it can get much colder in locations such as Siberia and Antarctica. Elsewhere in the Solar System there are places that make Antarctica seem scorching. And in laboratories, scientists can create temperatures so cold that even atoms nearly freeze up.

1 Maximum chill

The coldest temperature possible is known as Absolute Zero. This is 0 Kelvin, or −459.67°F (−273.15°C). At this temperature atoms have no energy at all and do not even vibrate.

3 Supercold boomerang

Temperatures near Absolute Zero might only be achieved in a lab, but there is at least one place in the Universe that comes pretty close. In a cloud of gas known as the Boomerang nebula, the temperature is thought to be just 1K (−457.87°F, or −272.15°C).

−273.15°C   **−272.15°C**

−459.67°F   **−457.87°F**

2 Coldest ever

In 2003, scientists cooled sodium gas inside a magnetic container to the coldest temperature ever achieved on Earth. It was just half a nanokelvin—half a billionth of a degree—above Absolute Zero!

MEASURING UP

Temperature is measured on three scales. In everyday life, people use degrees Fahrenheit (°F) or degrees Celsius (°C). You can convert from °F to °C using a simple formula: subtract 32, divide by 9, and multiply by 5. To convert from °C to °F, divide by 5, multiply by 9, and add 32. Scientists may prefer to use the Kelvin scale, which is identical to Celsius but starts at a different place. While 0°C is the freezing point of water, 0K (−459.67°F, or −273.15°C) is the lowest temperature possible and is called Absolute Zero.

Chilled matter

Substances normally exist in one of three states—gas, liquid, or solid—depending on the temperature. But at 17 nanokelvins above Absolute Zero scientists can push gases into another state, known as a Bose-Einstein condensate (BEC). In a BEC, atoms have so little energy that if a beam of light is passed through them then it will come to a complete standstill.

▶ Ultracold rubidium atoms (top) briefly condense into a BEC (center) before evaporating again (bottom).

Inside this flask, helium gas has been cooled to the point where it turns liquid.

▶ Antarctica experiences the coldest natural temperatures on Earth.

Ice station

The coldest outside temperature ever recorded on Earth was −128.6°F (−89.2°C) at the Russian Vostok Station in Antarctica on July 21, 1983.

4 Helium liquefies

Helium remains a gas until incredibly low temperatures. It finally becomes a liquid at 4K (−452.2°F, or −269°C).

7 Brrrr!

On February 6, 1933, the temperature in one of the world's coldest towns, Oymyakon, in Siberia, plunged to a bitterly cold −90 °F (−67.7°C).

−269°C	−235°C	−89.2°C	−67.7°C	0°C
−452.2°F	−315°F	−128.6°F	−90°F	32°F

5 Icy moon

The coldest place in the Solar System is Neptune's moon, Triton. It is so far from the Sun that it receives none of its heat, and temperatures on its surface drop to −315°F (−235°C).

▼ Uniquely, water expands when it freezes, making it less dense, which is why icebergs float.

Neptune

Triton

Freeze!

Water normally freezes solid to become ice at 273.15K (32°F, or 0°C). The addition of salt or pressure keeps it liquid at slightly lower temperatures.

Super SCORCH

The more energy things have, the hotter they get. Our bodies get their warmth from the energy released by reacting chemicals. The Sun and stars get their immense heat from the energy released when atoms are forced together by the tremendous pressures in their cores.

▶ Beneath the pale clouds, the surface of Venus is almost hot enough to melt tin.

3 On the boil

A liquid's boiling point is the hottest it can get without becoming a gas. The boiling point of water is normally 212°F (100°C). Beneath geysers, underground pressure allows water to be "superheated" to higher temperatures.

4 Trapped heat

Venus' thick atmosphere traps the Sun's heat, causing temperatures on the planet's surface to reach 896°F (480°C).

37°C	41°C	100°C	480°C	827°C
98.6°F	106°F	212°F	896°F	1,521°F

▲ This thermogram is created using infrared radiation. It indicates differences in temperature by color, from hot (white) to cool (blue).

2 Hot spots

In Dallol, Ethiopia, maximum daily temperatures averaged more than 106°F (41°C) for six years between 1960 and 1966!

5 Hot coals

The temperature of coal fires can vary, but coal can burn at up to 1,521°F (827°C).

1 Body heat

Your body temperature is normally around 98.6°F (37°C), except when you have a fever. Even then it only reaches 104°F (40°C)—much hotter would kill you.

◀ These sulfurous volcanic pools lie in a region that experiences some of the hottest temperatures on Earth: Dallol, in Ethiopia.

6 Molten metal

The bonds between atoms in a metal are very strong, so most metals don't melt until they get very hot. Some steels melt at around 1,517°F (825°C), while tungsten doesn't melt until around 6,170°F (3,410°C).

8 Blue star

The hottest known star in the Universe is Eta Carinae. Its surface reaches more than 72,000°F (40,000°C), which is why it glows blue-hot.

10 Hottest ever

In February 2010, scientists working deep underground in New York, U.S., in the tunnels of the Brookhaven National Laboratory's RHIC (Relativistic Hadron Ion Collider) created the hottest temperatures since the beginning of the Universe. In the RHIC's tunnels, gold atoms smash into each other at almost the speed of light, briefly creating temperatures of 7 trillion°F (4 trillion°C).

▼ In 2005, astronomers realized that superhot Eta Carinae is not one star but two.

3,410°C   5,500°C   40,000°C

6,170°F   9,900°F   72,000°F

▼ The Sun's atmosphere, or corona, reaches a blistering 1,800,000°F (1,000,000°C).

7 Sun burned

The temperature on the surface of the Sun is about 9,900°F (5,500°C). This extreme heat gives sunlight its yellow color—if the Sun were cooler, it would be more reddish. At the center of the Sun, temperatures reach more than 24 million°F (15 million°C)!

9 Big Bang heat

The hottest natural temperature was at the very start of the Universe, during the Big Bang, when temperatures briefly reached 3–5 trillion°F (2–3 trillion°C).

▶ Variations in microwave radiation in this computer map of the sky reveal the lingering glow of the Big Bang.

GIGANTIC Universe

To us tiny humans, Earth seems pretty big. A few centuries ago people thought it was the biggest thing in the Universe. But as telescopes reveal more, it's becoming clear that Earth is seriously small. Some things in space are so huge, they make our entire galaxy seem like a grain of sand on a beach.

Earth

Jupiter

1 Biggest planet

At 142,984 km across, Jupiter is the biggest planet in the Solar System. Its diameter is 11.2 times larger than Earth, and its volume is 1.43×10^{15} km³, so you could cram over 1,300 Earths inside Jupiter and still have room to spare!

Earth's diameter is 12,756.1 km. The volume of Earth is 1,083,210 million km³.

Earth

Sun

Jupiter

2 The Sun

The Sun dwarfs Jupiter. It is 1.4 million km across—109 times bigger than Earth. Its volume is $1,412 \times 10^{16}$ km³, which means you could get 1.3 million Earths inside the Sun.

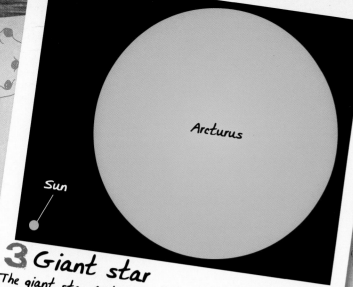

Sun

Arcturus

3 Giant star

The giant star Arcturus is 25 times the diameter of the Sun, and is the third brightest star in the night sky.

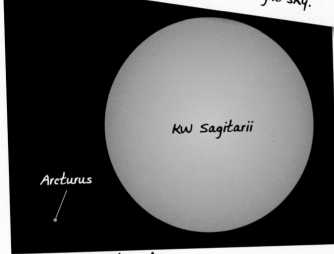

Arcturus

KW Sagitarii

4 Biggest star

The biggest star we know of is the hypergiant KW Sagitarii. At almost 2 billion km across it is 60 times bigger than Arcturus and more than 1,500 times bigger than the Sun!

LIGHT-YEARS

Dimensions in space are so vast that it's not practical to measure them in kilometers. Instead, astronomers measure things in light-years. Light always travels at the same speed—299,792 km/sec—so distances can be measured by the number of years it takes for light to cross them. A light-year is the distance light travels in a year, which is 9,460 billion km.

Milky Way galaxy

If the Sun were the size of a grain of sand, the Milky Way would be the size of the Sun!

5 Our galaxy

Our Sun is just one of about 400 billion stars in the Milky Way galaxy. The Milky Way is 100,000 light-years across—a million trillion km.

6 Biggest galaxy

The IC 1101 galaxy is 5 million light-years across—50 times as big as the Milky Way.

7 Supercluster

The Milky Way is one of more than 2,000 galaxies in the cluster of galaxies known as the Virgo Cluster. But this cluster is tiny compared with superclusters such as the Perseus-Pisces supercluster, which is more than 300 million light-years across—3,000 times as wide as the Milky Way. If the Sun were the size of a grain of sand, this supercluster would be almost as big as the Solar System.

8 Sloan Great Wall

The Universe is arranged like a gigantic spider's web. All the stars, galaxies, and clusters are concentrated in vast, thin walls. The biggest is the Sloan Great Wall, which is 1.37 billion light-years long—more than 12,000 times as wide as the Milky Way.

Mega IDEAS

As scientists explore the extremes of our world, they often need to use huge, complex pieces of equipment. Exploring the vastness of the Universe requires massive telescopes and research stations in space. Strangely, some of the biggest and most elaborate machines have been built to study things that are so tiny, they are invisible to the naked eye.

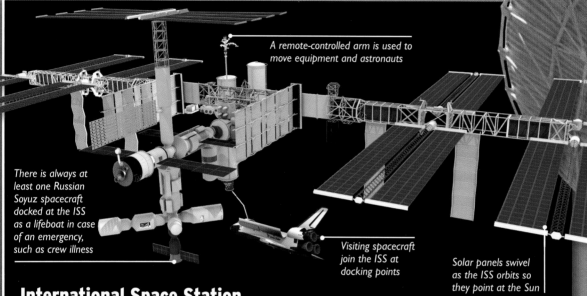

A remote-controlled arm is used to move equipment and astronauts

There is always at least one Russian Soyuz spacecraft docked at the ISS as a lifeboat in case of an emergency, such as crew illness

Visiting spacecraft join the ISS at docking points

Solar panels swivel as the ISS orbits so they point at the Sun

International Space Station

The biggest space station ever built, the ISS orbits between 173 mi (278 km) and 286 mi (460 km) above Earth. It is so big, it can be seen from the ground with the naked eye. Its parts were carried up bit by bit by dozens of space flights, then assembled in space by astronauts in more than 130 separate space walks.

▲ The ISS hurtles around Earth at an average speed of 17,239.2 mph (27,743.8 km/h), completing 15.7 orbits per day.

Human Genome Project

Every cell in your body carries instructions to keep you alive (and create your children), all contained on a tiny string of the chemical DNA. The instructions are in the form of thousands of chemical sequences called genes. The Human Genome Project was a huge international program to map the human genome (identify exactly where on human DNA every single gene occurs). The project began in 1990 and was completed in 2003.

▲ A computer image shows a tiny part of the map of DNA, with each bar showing one of the four chemical bases that make up the code.

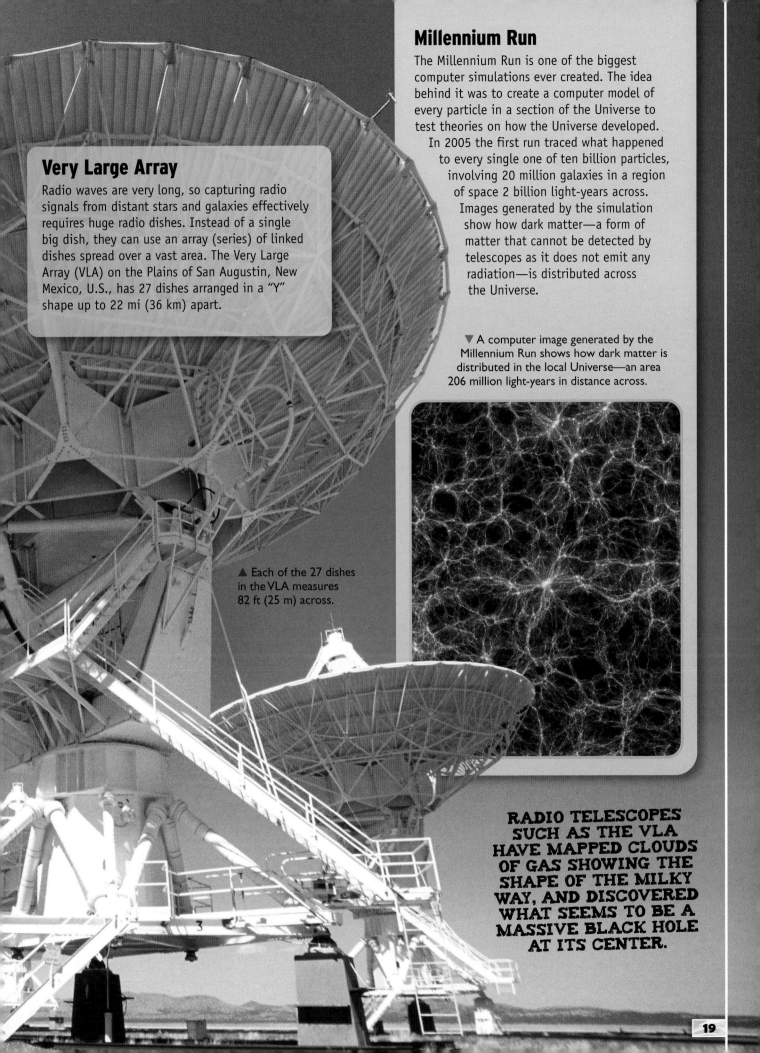

Very Large Array

Radio waves are very long, so capturing radio signals from distant stars and galaxies effectively requires huge radio dishes. Instead of a single big dish, they can use an array (series) of linked dishes spread over a vast area. The Very Large Array (VLA) on the Plains of San Augustin, New Mexico, U.S., has 27 dishes arranged in a "Y" shape up to 22 mi (36 km) apart.

Millennium Run

The Millennium Run is one of the biggest computer simulations ever created. The idea behind it was to create a computer model of every particle in a section of the Universe to test theories on how the Universe developed. In 2005 the first run traced what happened to every single one of ten billion particles, involving 20 million galaxies in a region of space 2 billion light-years across. Images generated by the simulation show how dark matter—a form of matter that cannot be detected by telescopes as it does not emit any radiation—is distributed across the Universe.

▼ A computer image generated by the Millennium Run shows how dark matter is distributed in the local Universe—an area 206 million light-years in distance across.

▲ Each of the 27 dishes in the VLA measures 82 ft (25 m) across.

RADIO TELESCOPES SUCH AS THE VLA HAVE MAPPED CLOUDS OF GAS SHOWING THE SHAPE OF THE MILKY WAY, AND DISCOVERED WHAT SEEMS TO BE A MASSIVE BLACK HOLE AT ITS CENTER.

Small WORLD

Looking at your skin through a magnifying glass reveals all kinds of details invisible to the unaided eye. However, scientists have now developed microscopes that allow us to see a world that is on a much smaller scale. Even a good magnifying glass only magnifies objects by a few times. The most powerful scanning tunneling microscopes (STMs) magnify things billions of times, and can reveal particles smaller than atoms.

Pepper

Salt

1 Salt and pepper

10^{-3} m (1 mm)

To the unaided eye, pepper looks pretty much like salt, only dark brown. But a good light microscope shows just how different they are. Pepper is, of course, the seed of a plant. Salt is a mineral crystal.

2 Human hair

10^{-4} m (100 micron)

Your hair may feel pretty smooth and fine, but under a microscope you can see that each hair has a rough surface, and looks rather like a tiny tree trunk.

3 Red blood cells

10^{-5} m (10 microns)

The most powerful light microscopes can show the tiny red cells in blood, but to see their shapes clearly you need a scanning electron microscope (SEM). SEM pictures show that when red blood cells are healthy, they are a neat button shape.

4 Bacteria

10^{-6} m (1 micron)
You can just about see bacteria with light microscopes, but SEM pictures can show detailed close-ups.

◀ Bacteria such as *Helicobacter pylori* live in many human stomachs, and can cause stomach upsets.

5 Virus

10^{-7} m (100 nanometers)
Viruses are much tinier than bacteria and can only be seen with electron microscopes, such as the transmission electron microscope (TEM).

Coronaviruses cause anything from colds to gastric illnesses. They got their name because they look like crowns through an electron microscope.

SCIENTISTS CAN MAKE ELECTRONIC DEVICES AS SMALL AS A SINGLE ATOM. VERY SOON, A POWERFUL COMPUTER NEED BE NO BIGGER THAN A GRAIN OF SAND.

6 Molecule

10^{-8} m (10 nanometers)
Atomic force microscopes (AFMs) and the most powerful TEMs can show actual strands of DNA.

◀ DNA can be seen clearly with a TEM, magnified almost half a million times.

7 Atom

10^{-9} m (1 nanometer)
To see an atom, you need a scanning tunneling microscope (STM).

MICROSCOPES

Light or optical microscopes use combinations of lenses to magnify things. They can magnify up to about 2,000 times. The smallest thing they can see is about 500 nanometers (500 billionths of a meter).

Electron microscopes can show things up to 20,000 times smaller. They don't use lenses at all—they fire electrons at their subjects and record the way the electrons bounce off. Instead of seeing an object directly, you look at a picture of it that builds up on a screen.

Scanning tunneling microscopes (STMs) and atomic force microscopes (AFMs) work by touch. AFMs run a sharp point that looks similar to an old-fashioned record needle over the subject. These microscopes can show atoms.

Microscopic
Zoo

In recent years, scanning electron and tunneling microscopes have homed in on the world of insects and microbes to reveal them in amazing detail and clarity. Even the tiniest bugs appear as large and monstrous as creatures from another world. There are many, many more different species of these microscopic organisms than there are in all the rest of the living world put together.

◄▲ A tiny fruit fly seen through an SEM with a close-up of the "talons" on its leg (inset left).

Small fly

Magnified more than 800 times, this SEM image shows the two birdlike talons on the end of a fruit fly's leg. The hairlike stalks beneath the talons are covered with adhesive pads or "pulvilli." These allow the fruit fly to cling to vertical surfaces such as glass, which appear completely smooth to the naked eye. Scientists are hoping to develop artificial nanomaterials that adhere in a similar way.

Stomach bug

Transmission electron microscopes (TEMs) reveal the microscopic zoo living inside the human stomach. This is the bacteria *Helicobacter pylori* magnified 7,700 times. These bacteria get their name, "pylori," from the fact that they live in the pyloric (lower) part of many people's stomachs. Fortunately, they usually have no effect.

▲ *Helicobacter pylori* can move around by whipping its tail or "flagella."

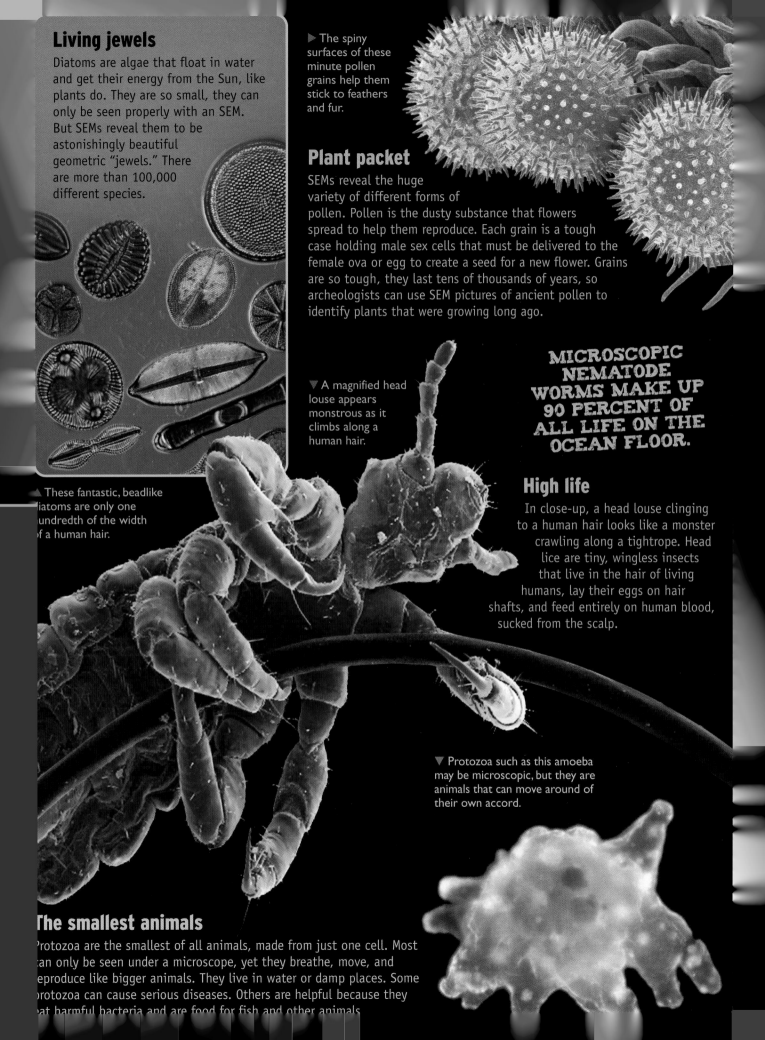

Living jewels

Diatoms are algae that float in water and get their energy from the Sun, like plants do. They are so small, they can only be seen properly with an SEM. But SEMs reveal them to be astonishingly beautiful geometric "jewels." There are more than 100,000 different species.

▶ The spiny surfaces of these minute pollen grains help them stick to feathers and fur.

Plant packet

SEMs reveal the huge variety of different forms of pollen. Pollen is the dusty substance that flowers spread to help them reproduce. Each grain is a tough case holding male sex cells that must be delivered to the female ova or egg to create a seed for a new flower. Grains are so tough, they last tens of thousands of years, so archeologists can use SEM pictures of ancient pollen to identify plants that were growing long ago.

▼ A magnified head louse appears monstrous as it climbs along a human hair.

MICROSCOPIC NEMATODE WORMS MAKE UP 90 PERCENT OF ALL LIFE ON THE OCEAN FLOOR.

High life

In close-up, a head louse clinging to a human hair looks like a monster crawling along a tightrope. Head lice are tiny, wingless insects that live in the hair of living humans, lay their eggs on hair shafts, and feed entirely on human blood, sucked from the scalp.

▲ These fantastic, beadlike diatoms are only one hundredth of the width of a human hair.

▼ Protozoa such as this amoeba may be microscopic, but they are animals that can move around of their own accord.

The smallest animals

Protozoa are the smallest of all animals, made from just one cell. Most can only be seen under a microscope, yet they breathe, move, and reproduce like bigger animals. They live in water or damp places. Some protozoa can cause serious diseases. Others are helpful because they eat harmful bacteria and are food for fish and other animals.

Light
FANTASTIC

In the last 50 years, scientists have come to understand light and radiation so well that they can now do things with it that might once have seemed like magic. The most exciting effects, such as the creation of holograms and measurements of astonishing accuracy, are achieved with laser light, but other kinds of light can be used for anything from seeing a living brain in action to spotting an invisible thumbprint at a crime scene.

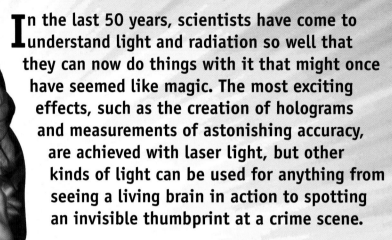

◀ A magnetic resonance image (MRI) scan "sees" inside a living body, showing both skeleton (white) and lungs (orange) in 3-D.

Body scan

Doctors and scientists use magnetic resonance imaging to take 3-D pictures that show the inside of the human body. It works by using powerful magnets to draw the nuclei (centers) of all the body's atoms into alignment. The magnet is then switched off. As the nuclei twist back to their normal position, they send out photons (particles of radiation). Detectors pick up the photons and a computer can then build up the 3-D image.

▼ This hologram shows Lindow man, a body preserved for 2,000 years in an English marsh.

Hologram magic

Holograms are 3-D images made by splitting a laser beam in two. One half, the reference beam, goes to the camera. The other bounces off the subject, breaking up the neat pattern of laser light waves. The camera records how this broken pattern interferes with (differs from) the reference beam, and this data can be used to project a 3-D image using lasers.

Nonmoving holograms have been around for half a century, but scientists are developing solid-looking moving holograms. In time, they may be able to create holograms that look like the real object.

▼ Ultraviolet (UV) light shows up otherwise invisible traces of blood and other body fluids splashed on a wall at a crime scene.

LASER LIGHT

The first laser beams were created in 1960 by Theodor Maimann. Laser light is like no natural light in the Universe. All natural light is said to be "incoherent" because it is a chaotic mix of lots of photons (particles of light) of different wavelengths. In laser light, the photons are all identical and in sync. The result is an intense beam of light of just one color, which is much harder to scatter than ordinary light. In fact, laser light can be bounced off the Moon and back and still stay in a single, tight beam.

Spotting the crime

Criminals may think they've left no trace of their crime, but ultraviolet (UV) light can reveal all kinds of invisible evidence. Fingerprints and traces of body fluids at the crime scene that cannot otherwise be seen show up clearly under UV—light made of waves slightly shorter than violet light, just too short to be visible.

Making stars

Shifting dust in the air makes it hard to get a clear view of space beyond. That's why stars appear to twinkle. Astronomers use computers to adjust telescope images for the dust, using bright stars as a reference—a technique known as Adaptive Optics (AO). But there aren't always bright stars in the part of the sky astronomers need to study, so instead they create their own guide star using a laser. As the laser is shone up into the sky it creates a little "star" where it hits sodium gas and makes it glow.

◄ An observatory sends out a beam of laser light to create a sodium laser guide star in the sky for astronomers.

Laser precision

The precision of a laser beam means it can be used to take incredibly accurate measurements. For example, geologists can bounce lasers off satellites to measure the distance between continents an ocean apart to within a few millimeters. LiDAR (Light Detection and Rangefinding) is an amazing way of building up an instant 3-D map, in which a survey plane or satellite moves over a target and scans it with pulses of laser light. Detectors then pick up the reflections and use them to build up a 3-D image.

Extreme
Conditions

Some scientists learn about the world in laboratories, but others venture into the most extreme conditions to gather data and make observations. To find out more, some scientists will fly into the heart of a hurricane, endure months in the bitter chill of the Antarctic, walk into an active volcano, crawl into deep caves, dive to the depths of the ocean, climb towering rain forest trees, and much more. Where there is something to be learned, scientists will go.

Hot and hazardous

Volcanoes are incredibly dangerous up close. Although a protective suit provides a shield against the heat and fumes, it will not save a person in the event of an eruption. The two most famous volcanologists (volcano experts) of all time, Maurice and Katya Krafft, were killed, along with 41 journalists, when they were filming on Japan's Mount Unzen in 1991. Without warning, the volcano blasted out an avalanche of searingly hot gas and ashes that engulfed them in seconds.

Volcanologists test material from a live volcano.

DANGEROUS DINNERS

Cooking in chemist Helen Maynard-Casely's kitchen is a dangerous business. She uses ordinary ingredients such as cream, sugar, and bread, but she subjects them to extreme pressures and temperatures to see what happens to them. She might chill cream with liquid nitrogen at −274°F (−170°C), or squeeze burnt toast hard enough to turn the carbon it contains into diamonds. Her colleague, Colin Pulham, at the Edinburgh Centre for Science Under Extreme Conditions, in Scotland, makes diamonds by blasting carbon with dynamite!

Scientists wearing breathing masks brave the poisonous air of a cave to collect samples.

Storm chasers

Tornadoes are incredibly powerful storms. Their twisting funnels of winds can blast a building apart or whip a truck into the air. But they are localized and very brief, rarely lasting more than 15 minutes. Scientists such as Chuck Doswell and Dr. Josh Wurman have to chase the tornadoes they study at high speeds—and risk being caught in the storm themselves. The chase is so exciting that many people now pursue tornadoes just for the thrill, but authorities fear someone may soon be killed.

Going underground

Professor Hazel Barton is willing to go into Earth's depths to pursue her studies of bacteria that live in extreme conditions. Bacteria such as these can only be found in the most inaccessible caves. To study them, Professor Barton has to squeeze through narrow passages and swim through underwater lakes where visibility is practically zero and the air is often poisonous.

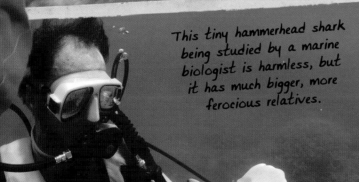

A storm chaser hurriedly sets down a weather probe in the path of an oncoming tornado.

The probe will measure conditions right in the heart of the tornado.

This tiny hammerhead shark being studied by a marine biologist is harmless, but it has much bigger, more ferocious relatives.

Ocean peril

Exploring the ocean can be difficult and even life threatening. In the surface waters, there is not only the danger of drowning, but also the threat of serious injury from potentially lethal creatures such as sharks, jellyfish, and stonefish. Deeper down, the water is bone-chillingly cold and pitch-dark—and the pressure is enough to crush a car.

Feel the FORCE

Force is what makes things happen. It can push things or pull them, speed them up or slow them down, draw them together or split them apart. Without forces, nothing would start or stop. Some forces—such as the force required to move your eye across this page—are tiny, while others are incredibly strong. Machines give us much more force than our bodies are capable of alone, but the most extreme forces are natural.

▼ The *Emma Maersk* dwarfs any passing craft, and is powered by an engine that weighs more than 2,500 tons.

Muscle cars

Power is a measure of not only force but also how fast it is delivered. A kilowatt (kW) of power is a force of one newton delivered at one meter every second. A small family car can get by with less than 50 kW of power, but to accelerate quickly, high-performance cars need a lot of force, very fast. That's why the *SSC Ultimate Aero TT*'s engine generates an incredible 960 kW of power.

Ship power

The more weight that must be moved, the more force you need, so the world's most powerful motors are on the world's heaviest ship—the *Emma Maersk*, which is driven through the ocean by the mighty Wärtsilä-Sulzer RTA96 diesel. It produces more than 83 megawatts (million watts) of power—as much as 10,000 high-performance cars!

MEASURING FORCE

One newton is the force that makes a mass of one kilogram accelerate at one meter per second every second. It's roughly equivalent to the force you'd use if you threw a big pebble into the sea.

45 N	The force required to push an adult over
670 N	The force of a karate chop breaking a plank
300–730 N	The gravitational force holding you on the planet
2,000 N	A good kick on a football
2,900 N	The force of a karate chop breaking a concrete slab
7,000 N	The force of an accelerating car
500,000 N	The force of a large locomotive
770,000 N	The thrust of a jumbo jet's engines
33,000,000 N	The thrust of the *Saturn V* rocket
200 million trillion N	The gravitational pull between the Moon and the Earth
350 billion trillion N	The gravitational pull between the Sun and the Earth

ONE OF THE STRONGEST FORCES EVER MADE BY HUMANS WAS FOR THE SATURN V ROCKET THAT LAUNCHED THE APOLLO SPACECRAFT TO THE MOON. THE FIRST STAGE OF THE ROCKET GENERATED A THRUST OF 3.4 MILLION N.

▼ The *SSC Ultimate Aero TT* is the most powerful sports car ever, and can reach a speed of more than 270 mph (430 km/h).

Fundamental forces

There are many kinds of force. "Contact" forces directly push or pull, for example when someone hits a ball. Others act "at a distance," with no direct contact. All the fundamental forces of the Universe—gravity, electromagnetism, and the two nuclear forces that hold atoms together—act at a distance. Forces like this depend inversely on the distance between the affected objects—that is, they get weaker the further apart they are.

Star quake

There are forces in the Universe that make anything on Earth look minuscule. On December 27, 2004, a flash of energy burst from the star SGR 1806-20 in what is called a "star quake." This quake had a power of 10,000 trillion trillion trillion watts. If the star had been even 10 light-years away from Earth it would have shaken the Earth to bits. Luckily, it was much further away!

▲ The energy burst from the star SGR 1806-20 in 2004 was so huge, it was visible from Earth.

◀ Buildings were sent crashing down by the San Francisco quake of 1989.

MOUNTAIN SHAKING

Even the thrust of a rocket such as the mighty *Saturn V* is dwarfed by the natural forces involved in earthquakes. The faintest tremor has 60 million watts of power, while the most powerful earthquake ever, which hit Chile in 1960, generated 11 million billion watts. With this kind of force, earthquakes can lift up and knock down entire mountains.

STRANGE Brains

Most scientists are sensible, rational people, but sometimes they are working on ideas too complictated for most regular people to understand, so they can come across as being a bit peculiar. A few scientists become so obsessed with their research that their behavior seems truly eccentric (to put it mildly). Here are a few of the strangest scientists ever.

Elixir of life

The German alchemist, physician, and theologian Johann Konrad Dippel (1673–1734) was convinced he could find an elixir that would give people eternal life—and bring dead people back to life. He lived in Castle Frankenstein in Germany and tales of his experiments with corpses inspired Mary Shelley's famous story of Doctor Frankenstein and his monster. Dippel also invented Prussian Blue, the first of the chemical dyes that are used to give most clothes their colors today.

▲ Johann Dippel thought he could find a liquid that would bring the dead back to life.

He's electric

Serbian-born American Nikola Tesla (1856–1943) was the genius who gave us our modern electricity supply by pioneering the use of Alternating Current (AC) to send power over huge distances. However, some of Tesla's theories were slightly more eccentric. His idea of transmitting energy through the air without wires is now becoming a reality, but thankfully his plans for a giant death ray have not come to fruition.

▶ Nikola Tesla's many unusual ideas included using magnetic coils to turn Earth into a huge steerable spaceship.

I CAN FLY!

Some of the bravest—or craziest—scientists have been those who attempted to fly. There are many who tried strapping on wings to jump from high places and never lived to tell the tale. One of the most daring and successful was German flier Otto Lilienthal (1848–1896). Lilienthal made more than 2,000 pioneering hang glider flights in the 1890s. Sadly, a flight in 1896 proved fatal, but his experiments were crucial to the Wright brothers' famous first plane flight seven years later in 1903.

▶ Otto Lilienthal in 1893 on one of his glider flights in the hills near Berlin, Germany.

▶ Kevin Warwick shows off the cyborg arm that responds to his thoughts.

The cyborg

Cyborgs are creatures of science fiction—they are half-human and half-robot. But British scientist Kevin Warwick (b. 1954) is turning himself into a cyborg for real. He isn't mad, though—he wants to experiment on himself to find ways of helping disabled people. He has implanted electronic devices into his arm that link his nervous system directly to a computer, so that he can operate the computer just by thinking.

ROCKET MAN

One of the pioneers of space technology, German-born American engineer Wernher von Braun (1912–1977) was obsessed with rockets from a very young age. Aged 12, von Braun packed his toy wagon with firecrackers and lit them, causing him to shoot across the street while his neighbors looked on in horror. The incident resulted in him being arrested by the police. However, von Braun was not so much mad as just dedicated to his science.

▶ Wernher von Braun was responsible for the development of the V2 rocket in Germany, and went on to become a leading figure in the American space program after World War II.

BLACK Hole

Black holes are places where gravity is so strong that it sucks everything in, including light. They form when a star or part of a galaxy gets so dense that it collapses under its own gravity, shrinking to an infinitely small point called a singularity. Gravity around the singularity is so ferocious that it sucks in light, space, and even time.

WE CAN'T STUDY THE POINT AT WHICH LIGHT DISAPPEARS IN A BLACK HOLE IN SPACE, BUT SCIENTISTS AT THE UNIVERSITY OF ST. ANDREWS, SCOTLAND, CREATED A VIRTUAL BLACK HOLE IN THE LABORATORY USING PULSES OF LASER LIGHT.

Old supernova

Some black holes form when an old giant star collapses into a supernova. Astronomers can't actually see black holes, but sometimes they can detect their presence from their effect on other objects. Stars often form pairs, or binaries. If one star is a black hole, astronomers might be able to see the effect of its gravity on the visible companion star. They may also spot X-rays bursting from matter ripped off the companion star by the power of the black hole.

▶ An artist's impression of a black hole (right) ripping matter off its companion star (left) in a binary pair.

Supermassive

In the center of the Milky Way, in a region called Sagittarius A*, 20 million stars are packed into a space just 3 light-years across, and hurtling round at incredible speeds. Calculations show they must be in the grip of the gravity of an object two to three million times as heavy as the Sun yet only twice as big. It must be what astronomers call a "supermassive black hole." There is thought to be one at the heart of every spiral-shaped galaxy.

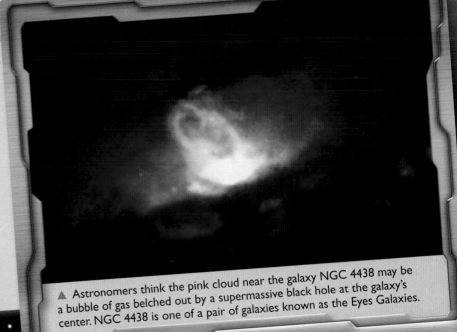

▲ Astronomers think the pink cloud near the galaxy NGC 4438 may be a bubble of gas belched out by a supermassive black hole at the galaxy's center. NGC 4438 is one of a pair of galaxies known as the Eyes Galaxies.

The powerful magnetic forces created by a black hole inside the galaxy Pictor A shoot out an X-ray jet thousands of light-years long.

Jet propulsion

Black holes don't just suck things in. As they mash up the matter they draw in, they can spew out giant jets of the remnants—electrons and other subatomic particles. The gigantic black hole at the heart of the M87 galaxy is shooting out an astonishingly brilliant beam of these remnants for thousands of light-years into the darkness, like some kind of galactic searchlight.

INSIDE A BLACK HOLE

In every black hole there is a point of no return, called the event horizon. Beyond this point, time has no meaning and not even light can get out.

If you saw someone falling into a black hole, you would never see them reaching the event horizon. Instead, you would see them going slower and slower and getting redder and dimmer until they finally faded away altogether.

If you fell into a black hole, you would be stretched out like spaghetti because the pull of gravity on your feet would be so much stronger than on your head. Astronomers believe you'd become so "spaghettified" that you would eventually be ripped apart.

As you are being ripped apart, time would speed up dramatically—you'd see the future flashing by outside the black hole. But you couldn't get out, or get a message out, since even light cannot escape a black hole.

Tunnel through time

Some scientists think black holes may be linked to white holes. White holes, if they exist, would be the opposite of black holes—places where matter and radiation spew out into space like a fountain. A few scientists think that black holes and white holes could be linked by a tunnel through space and time called a wormhole. If there are such things as wormholes, it might be possible to slip through them to travel vast distances through space instantly, or even to travel through time to the future or the past.

A MASSIVE Mystery

Deep beneath the countryside on the border of Switzerland and France is a circular tunnel more than 16 mi (27 km) long. Inside it is the world's largest machine—the Large Hadron Collider (LHC). It is basically a long, ring-shaped tube in which hadrons (subatomic particles) are accelerated round and round, reaching incredible speeds, and then smashing together. What scientists hope to see in the smashed bits may answer fundamental questions about the Universe, such as why things have mass, momentum, and inertia.

▼ The LHC has to run at incredibly low temperatures. This is the refrigeration or cryogenics unit.

▶ This computer simulation of the detector screen in the LHC shows what may happen if a Higgs boson (see far right) is found, sending out a spray of subatomic particles as it breaks up.

◀ The LHC uses powerful magnets to accelerate particles through a tube in opposite directions at high speeds and then smash them together head-on. Special sensors track the new particles created briefly as the smashed particles break up.

▼ A crash test shows the effects of momentum dramatically—the car starts to crumple just before the test dummy is catapulted forward.

INSURANCE INSTITUTE FOR HIGHWAY SAFETY
99 SUBARU FORESTER
CF98018

THE SEARCH FOR THE HIGGS BOSON

Forces such as electromagnetic radiation are transmitted by tiny "messenger" particles known as bosons. But scientists don't really know what mass is, or why things have inertia and momentum. It may all be down to a particle called the Higgs boson. This is how it might work:

Imagine a celebrity arriving at a party. As she swans in, fans (the Higgs bosons) crowd round her, giving her mass. The crowd makes it hard to get her moving, so she has inertia, but once they all start moving it's hard to stop them, so they give her momentum, too.

The mysterious Higgs boson is one of the things scientists are hoping to see among the smashed bits of particles in the LHC.

Momentum

Once an object is moving, it won't stop unless forced to because its mass propels it on. This is called momentum. It's what keeps the planets orbiting the Sun, and what carries a speeding roller coaster up the next incline. There's no more convincing demonstration of momentum in action than a crash test. When the test car slams into a wall, the momentum of the car and the dummy try to carry them on, which is why they smash into the wall with such force.

Inertia

It takes force to get something moving, because an object's mass keeps it rooted to the spot. This is called inertia. That's why a shot-putter has to be so strong to get the heavy shot moving.

◀ In order to throw the heavy shot, the shot-putter has to overcome all its inertia.

Mass

Momentum and inertia both depend on mass—the amount of matter involved. The heavier something is (the more massive it is), the more momentum and inertia it has.

Energy UNLEASHED

The nucleus of most atoms is fairly stable—but not always. Sometimes nuclei can partly disintegrate (radioactivity) or split in two (nuclear fission). Under severe pressure, different nuclei may fuse together (nuclear fusion). When any of these things happen, it unleashes matter and energy, known as radiation. The Universe is filled with natural radiation, and it's the energy of nuclear fusion that makes stars shine. Humans have learned to harness this energy, both to generate power and to create nuclear bombs—the most devastatingly powerful weapons of all time.

Solar power

The Sun shines because it is so big that the pressure in its core is huge—enough to force the nuclei of hydrogen atoms to fuse to make helium. The energy released by each individual fusion may be tiny, but there are so many atoms involved that the heat generated is enormous. This nuclear fusion drives temperatures in the Sun's core to 27 million°F (15 million°C) and makes the surface glow white-hot.

RADIOACTIVITY

The nucleus of an atom is made of two kinds of particle—protons and neutrons—and there are three main kinds of radioactivity:

Alpha decay is when an alpha particle (two neutrons and two protons) breaks away from the nucleus.

Beta decay is when a neutron splits to form a proton, emitting a beta particle (an electron) and a particle called an antineutrino.

Gamma rays are not emitted from the nucleus, but are a kind of electromagnetic radiation emitted from electrons like light, but they are very energetic and dangerous.

NUCLEAR FISSION

Conventional fuel is too bulky for submarines to carry for long voyages underwater, so many big subs are now powered by nuclear reactors. The reactors generate heat from the fission (splitting) of uranium atoms, which are large and easily split. The heat creates steam to drive the submarine's turbines. Just a few small rods of uranium fuel power a sub for many long voyages.

◄ Nuclear power allows submarines to stay on patrol underwater for long periods.

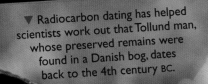

▼ Radiocarbon dating has helped scientists work out that Tollund man, whose preserved remains were found in a Danish bog, dates back to the 4th century BC.

Carbon dating

Some variations of atoms, called isotopes, are more likely to disintegrate radioactively than others. The radioisotope carbon-14, for example, is present in all living things, but when they die, the isotopes begin to disintegrate. The rate of disintegration is so steady that by measuring the proportion of carbon-14 isotopes left in remains of once living things, scientists can tell exactly how long they have been dead. This process is called radiocarbon dating and it is one of the most valuable archeological techniques.

▶ Thermonuclear bombs use a small fission bomb to set off a massive hydrogen fusion bomb. It starts with a gigantic fireball, such as this one in a test in the Pacific in 1958.

H-bomb

The nuclear bomb that destroyed Hiroshima in Japan in 1945 depended on the fission of big atoms such as uranium and plutonium. But even more terrible bombs were created by the fusion of tiny hydrogen atoms. The hydrogen was encased in a small bomb that was exploded first to create the pressure to fuse the hydrogen atoms. These hydrogen or H-bombs are now known as thermonuclear weapons.

Radiation danger

Exposure to radiation can be very dangerous. Gamma radiation is the most dangerous because the particles are small enough to penetrate the skin. The larger particles of alpha and beta radiation are less immediately dangerous, but if you eat any food containing them, they can also cause illnesses from nausea to cancer, and may even result in death.

◀ The accident at the Chernobyl Nuclear Plant, Ukraine, in 1986 was one of the worst ever, releasing radiation that was carried by wind far across Europe. The red color in this satellite image of the area around the nuclear plant indicates radioactivity.

Birth of the UNIVERSE

	10^{27} °C		10^{12} °C
	10^{-32} sec		3 min

0 seconds
First the Universe was a tiny hot ball that grew as big as a football, then cooled to (just) 10 billion billion billion°C.

10^{-43} seconds
In the "Planck" era, the four basic forces (gravity, electromagnetism, and the two nuclear forces) were joined as a single force.

10^{-12} seconds
The Universe became a sea of particles such as quarks and gluons, which began to gain mass.

10^{-32} seconds
The forces split into four and space swelled quadrillions of times in less than a fraction of a second, from something smaller than an atom to bigger than a galaxy. This is known as inflation.

3–20 minutes
Gravity and the other forces began to pull things together. Quarks and gluons joined to form the nuclei of the smallest atoms, hydrogen. Then hydrogen nuclei joined to make helium nuclei.

300,000 years
The first atoms formed and made gases.

One million years
After one million years or so, the gases began to curdle like sour milk into long strands called filaments with vast dark holes called voids in between.

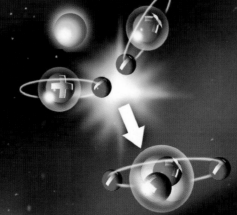

Galaxies are flying out and away from each other in all directions. This means the Universe must be expanding rapidly, so in the past it must have been much smaller. Indeed, it is now thought that long ago—about 13.5 billion years ago—the Universe was tinier than an atom. That was when it burst into being in what is often called the Big Bang. After the Big Bang, the Universe began swelling with such force and speed that astronomers are not sure if it will ever stop.

2,726 °C	253.15 °C	−270 °C
300,000 years	1 billion years	Today (13.7 billion years)

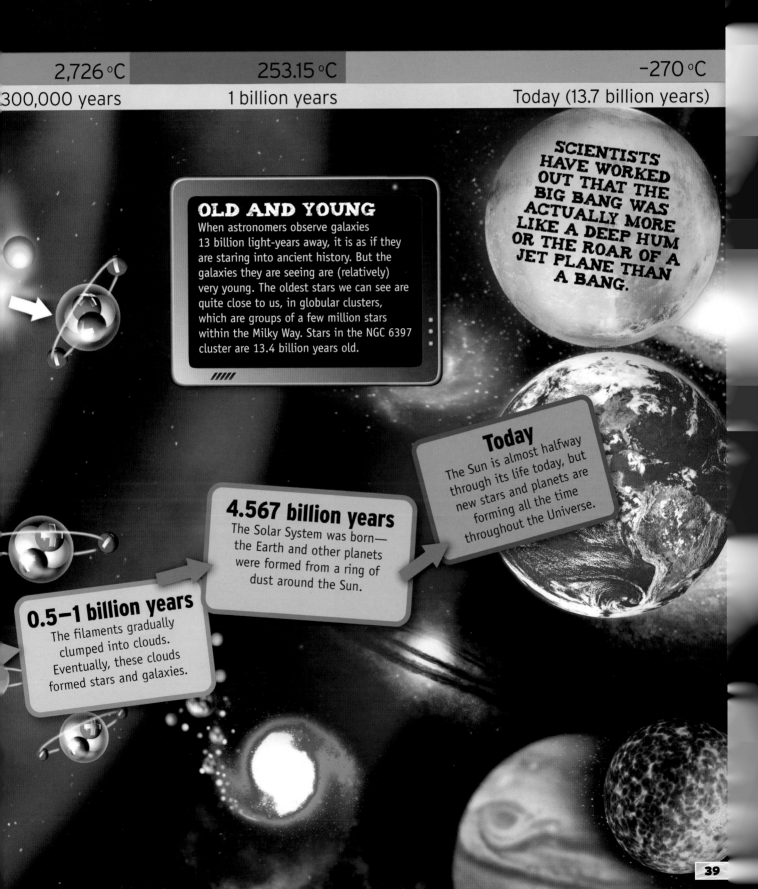

OLD AND YOUNG

When astronomers observe galaxies 13 billion light-years away, it is as if they are staring into ancient history. But the galaxies they are seeing are (relatively) very young. The oldest stars we can see are quite close to us, in globular clusters, which are groups of a few million stars within the Milky Way. Stars in the NGC 6397 cluster are 13.4 billion years old.

SCIENTISTS HAVE WORKED OUT THAT THE BIG BANG WAS ACTUALLY MORE LIKE A DEEP HUM OR THE ROAR OF A JET PLANE THAN A BANG.

Today
The Sun is almost halfway through its life today, but new stars and planets are forming all the time throughout the Universe.

4.567 billion years
The Solar System was born— the Earth and other planets were formed from a ring of dust around the Sun.

0.5−1 billion years
The filaments gradually clumped into clouds. Eventually, these clouds formed stars and galaxies.

INDEX

Entries in **bold** refer to main subject entries; entries in *italics* refer to illustrations.